Promotional Product

Selling

Part 2

Get results with this how-to-guide to selling in the
promotional product world.

Delia Biljon

Acknowledgements:
I would like to thank Nichole Van Wyk for her assistance with this book. It is always a pleasure to work with someone so knowledgeable.

Author
Delia Biljon
P.O. Box 51243
Musgrave
Durban
South Africa
4062

Contents

Promotional Products Industry Overview

- ❑ The birth of the industry was the late 1800's
- ❑ Today, the promotional industry is worth $15.64 billion in sales.

INDUSTRY SALES VOLUME IN BILLIONS

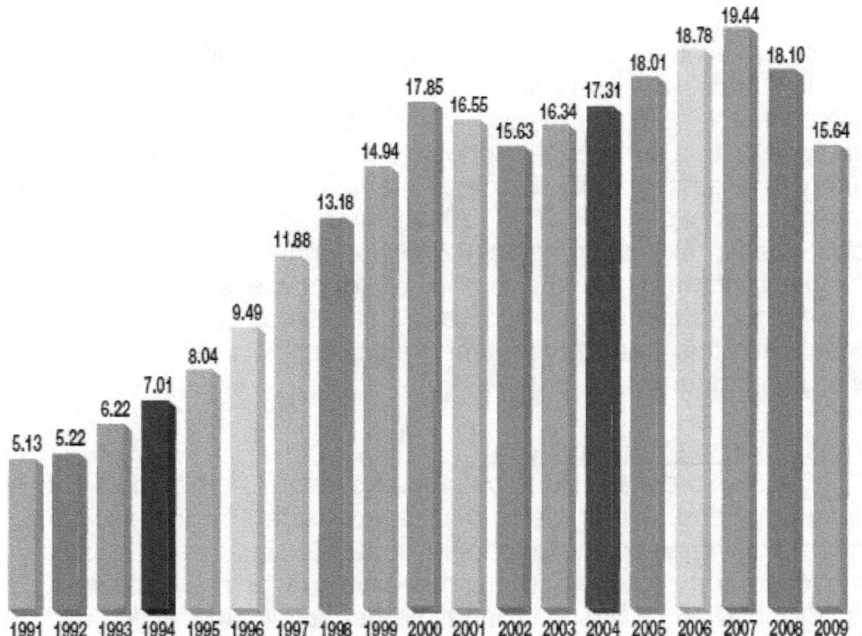

Data source: Information from the Promotional Products Association International (PPAI - 2009)

Definition:

Promotional products comprise useful items that are used in marketing and communication programs. The items include wearable's, writing instruments, calendars, drink ware and many other items, usually imprinted with a company's name, logo or message.

Overview

Distributor sales of promotional products in the US declined by 13.61% in 2008 to $15 638 571 468. This is the lowest since 2002 and the sales volume is a direct reflection of the tough economy that affected advertising media across the board in 2009. Although there is no data available in South Africa regarding the promotional product sales, key suppliers have noted a clear decrease in sales in 2009 due to the economy both internationally and locally. The global financial crisis wiped out a number of economies so it is no surprise that the industry took a hit in 2009. Larger companies in the US experienced smaller decreases in sales (2.35%) while smaller companies experienced a huge decrease of 22.62%. A number of printing, packaging and health supply companies (dental, eye care, medical and veterinary supply) now report significant sales in promotional products and this could account for the smaller decrease in sales by the larger companies.

Comparisons to other media

A 13.6% sales drop isn't good but in comparison to other media, it looks pretty good. Other media that saw considerable losses were print advertising, with newspapers losing 28.6% in advertising sales and consumer magazine and revenue dropping 18.1%. Billboard sales dropped 15.6% last year and internet advertising, which had been growing in double digits in recent years, was down 3.4%. The biggest surprise was a 15.6% drop in sales for direct mail, which hadn't had a loss in modern times until now. Although the drop in sales for other media doesn't make matters better, it does help us to know that the drop in promotional product sales was not abnormal.

Purpose of research

The Promotional Product Association International has been trying to secure data on the annual sales of distributors since 1965. The information is used primarily to gauge international trends and to measure industry growth. There is no data available in South Africa to draw on.

Beyond 2010

Companies must realise that they have to keep marketing to get through the economic difficulties. Distributors must bear in mind that they not only provide advertising but also tools, strategies and even execution to motivate, incentivise and influence business relationships, they are part of a bigger picture that extends beyond calling attention to a product.

To acquire and keep customers requires more sophistication in terms of understanding client's concerns and problems – including how end users will react to receiving a particular promotional product.

Selling solutions, not just products, is the key to making it in today's market.
There are shifts occurring in the communications and media industry and this industry is poised to become a very large sector. Most of this growth will be in communications that deliver relevancy and impact – an incredible opportunity for innovators in the promotional products industry to excel.

Top Promotional Product Categories

These products make up 73% of industry sales (data: PPAI – 2009)

- ❑ 31% Wearable's
- ❑ 10% Writing Instruments
- ❑ 7% Bags
- ❑ 6% Drink ware

- ❑ 6% Desk and Office Accessories
- ❑ 6% Calendars
- ❑ 4% Recognition Awards/Trophies/Jewellery
- ❑ 3% Computer related accessories

Top Buyers of Promotional Products

(Data: PPAI – 2009)
- ❑ Education
- ❑ Financial
- ❑ Non Profit
- ❑ Healthcare
- ❑ Construction
- ❑ Trade & Professional Associations
- ❑ Real Estate
- ❑ Government
- ❑ Professionals
- ❑ Restaurants & Bars

Top Uses of Promotional Products

(Data: PPAI – 2009)
- ❑ Customer goodwill and retention
- ❑ Tradeshows
- ❑ Employee relations and events
- ❑ Brand awareness
- ❑ Public relations
- ❑ New customer / account generation
- ❑ Employee service awards
- ❑ Non profit programs
- ❑ Internal promotions
- ❑ New product / service introductions

Why Promotional Products Work

Promotional products are:

- Useful
- Appreciated by the recipients
- Retained by the recipients
- Repeatedly displaying the clients message at no additional cost per impression

Promotional products furnish advertisers with additional advantages that may not be available in other media such as high recall, creating a favourable impression of the advertiser, promotional products are generally retained for a long period of time, recipients are more likely to recommend the advertiser and they create a positive overall impression.

The Evolution of Promotional Sales

Product peddler – Idea generator – Program creator – Promotional consultant

Don't be a product peddler and give your client a catalogue to choose items that they like and then give them the best price. Be an idea seller / an idea generator and give them a program that ADDS VALUE.

Selling Methods

Proactive
- Telemarketing / email
- Cold calling
- Warm calling
- Appointments
- Scheduled visits

Reactive

- ❏ Answer the phone
- ❏ Check the email

Being proactive is very important. Be the hunter and not the farmer (the hunter seeks new accounts and the farmer maintains the accounts but does not look for new business). Take at least a day each week and get new accounts THEN maintain them and get new business from those existing accounts.

Price, Quality and Service
- ❏ Value at overlap
- ❏ Adjust value to fit need

Price

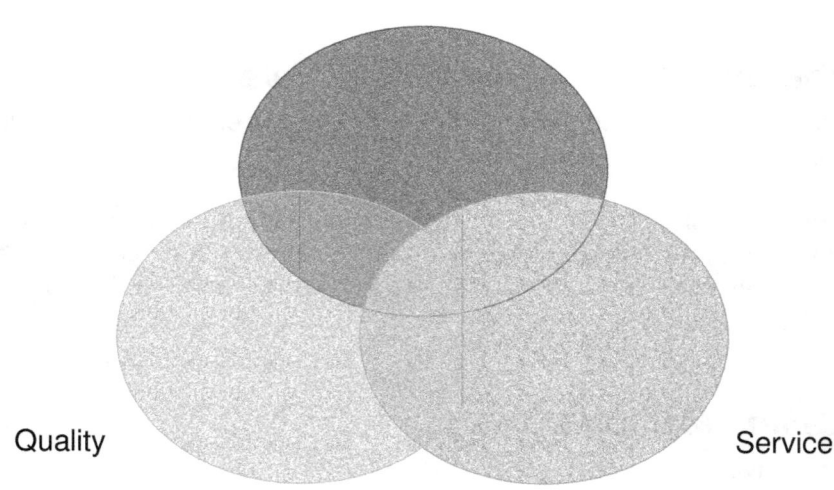

Quality

Service

Bear in mind that you can not give the best price, best quality and the best service. You can not be all things to all people but you can try to adjust the price, service and quality according to the customers needs until the value in the middle overlaps and that is what you should focus more on. Examples may be:
- ❑ Board meeting gift – quality will be important
- ❑ Give away on the street – price will be important
- ❑ Deadline – service will be important

You will need to adjust the diagram according to what the customers needs are and that will be the focus for that customer at that time.

How do you interface with your client?
- ❑ Professional buyer on your clients behalf
- ❑ Provide client with a marketing vehicle to carry his message
- ❑ Consult with and council your client
- ❑ Provide your client with a total marketing solution
- ❑ Add value such as warehousing fulfilment, decorative services, gift wrapping, event and trade show services, program development

What is a PROGRAM?

A program is a systematically executed promotional products campaign that is designed to motivate a target audience to achieve a desired goal. You concentrate on solutions rather than tangible objects. You will have to gain a good understanding of your client's needs, objectives and attitudes and this will lead to further dependence on you and a natural desire to consult you on new programs.

Types of programs
Dealer / distributor
Safety incentive
Employee service awards and recognition
Sales motivation

Company store
Casual day / uniform
Direct mail

How do you become such an expert?
You do not become an expert in program selling overnight. Begin by being a good sales person, alert to the needs of your customers, concerned with the results of every campaign in which you have a part. Observe carefully how promotional products help fill your customers needs. You will begin to be less of an order taker and more of an advisor, ready to recommend what to buy and how to use it to meet a marketing need. Understanding your customers marketing problems is essential. As you begin to work regularly with a client, show a concern for the way in which promotional products are used. Remember a promotional product is not an end in itself. It is bought to help achieve a specific objective and to solve a specific problem. To do this effectively, the article must not only be appropriate, but also be distributed to the right audience, with the right message, in the right package, at the right time.

You should be concerned about these surrounding elements, because the success of your sale depends on them. Once you have developed this broad concern, you have laid the groundwork for program selling.

Program selling requires more than just selling promotional products to achieve a goal but as mentioned in part 1 of this series, you need to start somewhere and selling promotional products is a good place to start. Once you have mastered selling promotional products, start selling ideas then program selling once you are confident.

Program opportunities
Admin
- ❑ Suggestions
- ❑ VIP business gifts
- ❑ Special events, sponsored charities
Manufacturing

- Safety
- Production goals
- Quality incentives

HR

- Employee recognition
- Employee recruiting, retention
- Service awards
- Company store
- Casual day / uniforms

Marketing and sales department

- Distribution chain incentives
- Sales incentives
- Customer loyalty

What do you need to know (qualifying questions)

- What is the goal of the program
- Clients budget
- Number of participants
- Participant demographics
- Expected distribution
- Marketing theme

Basic steps to follow in program selling:

1. Define specific objectives.

   This is the first and most important step in defining and designing an incentive based program. Often program needs arise from casual conversations with clients or prospects who think they have no program requirements. Simply ask: "What do we want to accomplish with this program?"

   Your objectives should specify:
   - What specifically is to be accomplished
   - How you plan to measure these activities
   - How the plan will help accomplish the goals
   - Targeted performance levels

❑ The timeline of the program, such as time allotted to reach objectives

2. Identify the audience to be reached.
Some programs will have one specific target, but many will include several audiences that you need to combine for maximum benefit. For example, a sales contest may be aimed specifically at the sales force, but also require the help of support people to make the desired objectives achievable. When designing a program, be sure you consider all stakeholders.

3. Agree on a budget.
Sometimes the budget will be handed to you by the client. Other times it needs to be developed based on what the program is meant to accomplish, what the economic payoffs of accomplishing the objectives will be, what the economic liabilities of not achieving the objectives will be, what has been done in the past, what funds are available now etc.

4. Determine a workable implementation plan.
The promotional plan might include:
❑ A pre-announcement teaser to generate curiosity about the program
❑ An announcement piece which explains how your audience can win
❑ Promotional mailings, signs, stickers, banners and specialities to stimulate interest and keep the program message alive
❑ Training materials
❑ A schedule of releasing updates and promotional pieces to provide increased message life and interest over the life of the program

❑ Ways to evaluate the progress and success of the program

5. Create a theme for the promotion.
The theme needs to fit the image of the organisation, the target audience, other on-going communication patterns within the organisation, and the objectives to be achieved. You may consider developing a theme mascot such as a cartoon character, to make the theme more tangible and interesting.

6. Develop promotional messages to support the theme.
Even promotions need promoting. If your promotional program is longer than three months you will need to provide a number of boosts to keep the theme fresh, interest high and on the minds of those in your target audience. These messages are best placed on promotional products.

7. Select the appropriate promotional products.
Ideally the products you select need to be appealing to the target audience and bear a natural relationship to the objectives, theme, message, etc. Contrary to product selling, the products are the last things selected for a program and can be selected from a very wide range of possibilities.

8. Establish a way of measuring results.
This step is extremely important. It provides the feedback you need to demonstrate the success of the program and to improve future programs. Plus, it is a ready-made answer to the question, "What have you done for me lately".

Tip:
Choose items based on the demographic and not on what you like.

Use the worksheet below to assist with qualifying questions

Promotional Planning Worksheet

What is our
business?
_____

What is our
corporate
image?
_____

What is our
product(s)
position in the
marketplace?
_____

_____

Our target
market is:
_____

Our market's
demographic
is:
_____

Items with
demographic
utility:
_____

What is the
message or
theme we want
to
communicate: _____

What is our
measurement
of success? _____

Reasons for
the campaign:

- ○ Tradeshow Giveaway
- ○ Safety Program
- ○ Public Relations
- ○ New Customer/Account Generation
- ○ Branch Opening
- ○ Employee Service Awards
- ○ Marketing Research

- ○ Brand Awareness/loyalty
- ○ Employee Event
- ○ Dealer/Distributor Relations
- ○ New Product/Service Introduction
- ○ New Location
- ○ Not for Profit Program
- ○ Incentives (sales, safety, education, quality, productivity, attendance, etc)

Item
Information:

Event Date: _____

Due Date: _____

Budget / Price
Range _____

Pieces
needed: _____

Imprint / Art: _____

colours /
positions: _____

Special
Packaging: _____

Shipping
Requirements _____

Other questions at an initial meeting to get the client thinking:
If you are at a networking function for example – ask probing questions:

- ❏ What events do you have coming up in the next 90 days?
- ❏ Do you currently use business gifts?
- ❏ What do you do to promote your business in the market place?
- ❏ Tell me about your employee incentive program.

If the prospect is still not interested – not a good prospect!

You can also dig deeper and ask:

- ❏ What do you do to motivate clients?
- ❏ Do you attend trade shows?
- ❏ What do you need to accomplish?

THE DIAGNOSTIC APPROACH: QUESTIONS ARE THE ANSWER

The Diagnostic Approach:
Examine the patient
Diagnose the problem
Prescribe the solution

Rapport Building Questions

1. What is the biggest sales and marketing issue you are dealing with right now?
2. Where do you need to see some quick improvement?
3. What sort of business gifts do you use?
4. What is the primary thing that you would like me to help you with?
5. What sort of events do you have coming up in the next 30, 60 and 90 days?
6. What are the biggest challenges you face in promoting your business right now?
7. What is the most effective promotion you have done?
8. What is the least effective promotion you have done?

Rapport Building Tools

1. Useful and targeted promotional products – get this on your customer's desk and tie the product into a message.
2. Email or printed newsletter – help people understand how to use promotional products to position their brand. Position your staff and yourself as an expert.
3. Audio and video pod cast – Read an email with a microphone or use a webcam and put post ideas to your website. Also send an email with that link.
4. Book on effective use of promotional products – give this to your clients or use quotes from the book.
5. Excerpts on books.
6. Gift related to client's interests or industry.
7. An interesting article you have written or read.
8. Random sample of an appropriate new product. Perhaps with your clients logo on it or even a virtual sample.
9. Details on a successful person you have read about.
10. A recommendation on a program that clients need and want.

DEVELOPING your proposal / marketing plan

The Marketing plan

Quantify client objectives
- ❏ Figure out what the client's objectives are, for example : How many new customers they want?

Quantify the client's financial benefit (Long Term Value or LTV of client)
To do this, you will need to ask some sensitive questions about their business so you can get a non-disclosure mutual agreement that will ensure privacy of this information.
- ❏ Calculate the clients needs
  1. How many clients do they have?
  2. What is their annual revenue?
  3. Take the revenue / total number of clients = annual revenue per client
  4. Annual average revenue X average years they keep a client = LTV
- ❏ Now calculate pre-tax value per client
  LTV x 20% (your companies average pre-tax profit) = pre-tax value

Example:

If your company has 100 clients and makes a gross annual revenue of R1, 000 000.00 per annum and the average time that you keep a client is 5 years. Your calculation would be:

Take the annual revenue (R1mil) x Average number of years that you keep your clients (5years) / the number of clients (100) = Long Term Value of that client (R50 000).

Now calculate the pre-tax value per client which will be the LTV or Long Term Value x whatever your companies' average pre-tax profit may be. In this example, we are using a net profit of 20%.

Pre-tax (20%) = Pre-tax LTV of R10000.

<u>Determine the client's objective</u>
Now discuss what return they want?
If the pre-tax value is R10000 and they want to double their money (100% return) then they can afford to spend R5000 per client. If they want to get 10 new clients then they can easily spend R50000 (R5000 x 10).

<u>Discuss meeting/exceeding and falling short of the client's objective</u>
Ask your client if they would be happy if you fell short of the objective by achieving a 50% return for example. Who wouldn't be happy with 50%? Find out if falling short would be acceptable and if so, what would be an acceptable range.

<u>Other questions to ask the client:</u>
Determine the message and call to action.
Determine the media that will deliver the message.
How and when will the results be measured?
Is there a mechanism to process the leads?
Fill out the "Promotional Planning Worksheet" on page 16.

Strategic Marketing

Now go away and develop your plan for the client. Answer the following questions:

- ❑ What are the client's objectives?
- ❑ Who makes up their target market?
- ❑ Where has the client been positioned by the market?
  Speak to the clients customers and ask them why they use the company? Why do they like them?
  Why do they not like them?
  (You will find out very quickly what your clients position is in the market place in the clients minds)

- ❑ Target market research, data collection and analysis
- ❑ Competitive assessment
  Take a yellow pages and look at dentists for example, look at the adverts in the newspaper or on websites and you will see what they are heading towards (analysis of the market)
- ❑ Create a marketing/advertising mix
  This does not only involve promotional gifts or clothing; arrange the event and outsource and make sure that you brand everything at that event. Outsource the golf day and you can do the 4 ball prizes, the banners, the clothing etc and have each and every item branded, even the table cloths and napkins.
- ❑ Measure the clients Return On Objective (ROO). Remember that it is better to measure the ROO as opposed to the Return On Investment (ROI) because we can not keep measuring the campaign 1 year later, the return on objective is far better to measure.
- ❑ Follow up and go for round 2.

Marketing our media vs. other media

Promotional companies are not an interruption! People love receiving promotional gifts. Try a marketing SMS – that is an interruption!
- ❑ Ours is a 19 billion dollar industry
- ❑ Our media is bigger than cable TV and outdoor advertising
- ❑ Promotional products can engage all five senses:
  Touch – weight or texture
  Sight – we can see the product
  Sound – the sound of the item (pen click for example)
  Smell – scented products
  Taste - branded chocolate

What Clients Want

Company Reputation
Not what we say – it is what we do

Sales Rep's Product Knowledge
Can't know everything about each of 700 000 products but must know where to go to find the product

Time Saving Benefit
Customer's time is valuable
We must save them time
Convey benefits to them
Think of ideas to grow their business

Ease of Contacting the Sales Rep
Be available and if voicemail, phone right back
Never wait until back in the office
Use technology to improve communication

Ability to Supply Custom Work
You must be a detailed person
Your ability to 'handle it' will be your biggest advantage
Take an idea from concept – finish/delivery and you will be better than competitors

Variety of Product Selection and Options
Provide 'intelligent' and thoughtful ideas
Too many options are not good
Provide samples
Have good suppliers with great products

Easy Access to Product and Price Info
It must be easy for the customer to get information from you
You must vouch for the product

Provide clients with better results than they can get on their own – if not walk away
15 cents for the competitor's pen – ask if it will write, will it be available, delivered on time?

All Charges Clearly Explained
Be clear upfront
Tell them the process
Tell about screen posies, overrun charges or shipping

Competitive Pricing
Cheaper is not the top issue to the client
It is not about the lowest pricing, it is about competitive pricing
Always assume what is in their best interest and yours – good quality products at a reasonable price, delivered on time by someone they like

Timely Response to Customer Concerns
Know what is happening every step of the way - let the client know!

If there is a problem:
Match client's intensity (they are concerned, you are concerned)
Say sorry – what is the problem
Position problem as unusual
Take ownership of problem
Follow up immediately – if you say you will call back in 30 minutes, call back in 20 minutes

Prompt and Timely Delivery of Orders
Get the right suppliers who won't let you down
If you can't, your business is doomed!

How Things Work – Leverage

Leverage: Getting maximum result from minimum effort.

Three key areas to leverage:
1. Time
2. money
3. relationships

Ideas on how I can better leverage my:

Time:
- Schedule appointments closely together.
- Schedule meetings geographically (don't waste time and effort by not doing this).
- Organise for productivity.

Money:
- Get deposits from customer (50%). Why deposit? We can do without a deposit but we have discovered over the years that if you don't have the money now, why would you have the money after supplying you. Great risk after the item is printed and can not be returned.

Relationships:
- Suppliers
- Prospects and clients – know them and their calendar. Be in front of prospects consistently.
- Bankers – unless you are getting paid, you're not in business.

GROWING YOUR CLIENT BASE PROACTIVELY

How do you want to grow your business?

- Geographically (horizontal selling)
  This is everyone in a chosen geographic area. Here you would sell to anyone who needs promotional items regardless of what industry or business they are in.

- By Industry (vertical/niche selling)
  This is by industry regardless of where they are situated. Learn everything about that market. Find out what they want to achieve and put a promotion together based on that. It is better to specialize and understand the needs of that market. The client will pay more for the knowledge from the promotional consultant.

- By Program Speciality
  Examples are safety programs, employee achievements, event marketing and trade show marketing.

- By Product Speciality
  These are trophies, wearables, gifts etc. There are quite a large range of products to choose from. You can choose one category or a combination of categories.

- Some Combination Thereof
  An example could be trophies (product) to karate schools (industry) world wide

WHICH INDUSTRIES WOULD YOU LIKE TO TARGET?

- Education
- Financial Institutions
- Non-Profit
- Health Care

- o Construction
- o Clubs and civic organizations
- o Real Estate: agents, title companies
- o Government
- o Professionals
- o Restaurants/Bars
- o Automotive
- o Insurance
- o Entertainment/Sporting Events
- o Media
- o Manufacturers
- o Hospitality
- o Computers/Software
- o Utilities
- o Freight and Delivery
- o Telecommunications
- o Agriculture
- o Retailers & Shopping Malls

Please take the time to do the following tasks:

Who's Spending Money Now?

1. List five industries you think you would like to target.
2. Under each, list the names of at least five companies from that industry in your market area.
3. Under each company name, list the names of the buyers from each department mentioned in the list program.

Note
Buyers within the company could be:
- ❖ Executives
- ❖ Administrative
- ❖ Advertising or marketing people
- ❖ Human resources

❖ Safety and compliance officers
❖ Purchasing department

FOUR WAYS TO GROW SALES AND PROFITS

MORE CLIENTS!

- Increase the number of clients:
  Prospect more and schedule a time each day to commit to doing this.

  Convert better – 1 in 10 ratio or 5 in 10?

  Implement a proactive referral system. Go out and get referrals from your best clients but ask the right questions; "Who do you know that needs help promoting their business?" or "Who do you know that needs to retain employees?"

MORE MONEY!

- Increase the average rand amount of each transaction.
  Always ask for more than you expect to get.

  Quality – give the best, for example a high quality mug with wrapped logos and a gold foiling executive mug. Start with a higher quality mug and then go lower. The law of psychology proves that you can go higher to lower if value is perceived but not from lower to lower value.

  Quantity – Have a minimum quantity. If a big customer would like a small quantity some of the time, that if fine but do not do business with less than minimum orders. Do you really want the headache of minimum orders for the same amount of running around?

Up-sell – Offer gifts for different level customers

Cross-sell – Offer something that goes with the order for example, if a client orders 100 t-shirts, offer 100 caps for an extra R... (they are already doing a logo so why not)

MORE MARGINS!

- Increase your profit margin. How?

Increase the amount that you charge your client

Decrease the amount that you pay your suppliers

Do both!

How?

Sell value to your customers. Establish good relationships with suppliers for better prices.

MORE OFTEN!

- Increase the frequency of purchases.

Get your clients to order more often.

How?

Learn your client's calendar. If the client has a show coming up in a few months, diarise this and ask if they would need banners or balloons. Always bear in mind that clients do not always remember exactly what you sell.

Plan for re-orders from the first sale. Ask how long it will take your client to go through this product. Tell them to consider giving the gift out to sales people to give out to customers for another reason. This way, they will go through the gifts quicker and re-order sooner.

Demonstrate YOUR value to your client.
Add value and always recommend solutions.
Be interesting and ask the client about themselves, they will end up thinking that you are interesting!

SELLING SOLUTIONS

- o <u>I want you to think for me, so I don't have to</u>.
  Your clients expect you to be the expert.
  People who know what they want are less valuable as they can go anywhere and shop for price. Show value!

- o <u>I want solutions to my business problems</u>.
  Growing business
  Keeping staff happy
  Finding more accounts
  Human Resources – make sure that staff come to work

  Clients will focus on particular things so find out what it is and give them solutions.

- o <u>I want you to tell me what works and what doesn't.</u>
  If a client's average order is R100 000.00 and the client wants to give out pens, recommend something more high end. Advise the client and this will help you in turn.

- o <u>I want to feel like I'm getting preferential treatment</u>.

An example here is if you don't have your cell phone number on your business cards, you can write your cell phone number down as you give the card to the client and they will feel really special.

○ <u>I want to feel that you understand my industry, or better yet, my business</u>.
You can put a promotion together if you know who buys from that client in that industry.

Promotional gifts have tremendous advantages:
Deliver low cost per impression vs. adverts
Delivers a gift
Delivers perceived value
Logo is seen as often as 5 times per day
If someone else sees the logo, the client is a walking billboard and there is a feeling that the client has endorsed that company buy using the item.

TITLES TO GIVE YOUR PROGRAMS

NEVER say to clients that you sell promotional gifts and corporate clothing. Rather say that:
"I help customers get more business"
"I help companies retain employees"

- Customer acquisition programs
- Customer retention programs
- Employee retention programs
- Revenue enhancement programs

TEN ACTION STEPS TO HIT THE GROUND RUNNING

1) Focus each day on delivering the fifteen criteria most important to promotional products clients. Place particular emphasis on items 1 through 5 to counteract price issues.

2) Use the leverage the industry provides to consistently outperform your competition.

3) Don't focus on selling products, focus on providing solutions. Event marketing, business gifts, self-promotion, etc. Be an advisor, not a distributor.

4) Build your business proactively. Target the businesses and industries that are likely to spend the most money with you.

5) Work every day on each of the four ways to grow your business: more clients, more money, more margins, more often!

6) Always structure your offers from high to low on quality, quantity and price.

7) Master the "diagnostic approach" by constantly fine tuning and asking rapport-building questions.

8) Use specific, pre-determined, rapport-building tools to establish your expertise, demonstrate your commitment and clearly define for your clients what sets you apart.

9) Track your leads, relentlessly and help your clients do the same. Train them to use promotional products as an integral part of the lead tracking process.

10) Live a little! Structure your business to work for you instead of the other way around.

POWER PROSPECTING

Eight Tips for Power Prospecting

1. **Continuously prospect your clients**
   Ask your clients these questions (if they answer yes to any of these then they are a good client but if they answer no, then move on):
   Can I offer?
   Event marketing
   Business gifts
   Self promotion tools
   Employee relations tools
   Trade show incentives

2. **Implement a referral system**
   Always ask your customers for a referral and keep it up.

3. **Always warm call before cold calling**
   Know who you will be visiting and give them a call first.

4. **Be certain your first contact suits you**

5. **When starting cold, work from the top down**
   Always call the CEO's office and you will no doubt encounter the "gatekeeper" which is actually the plan. Ask who the appropriate person is to contact for promotional items. Get the gatekeepers name and when you call the person say that the gatekeeper referred you. The gatekeeper will have no problem referring down because her only job is to screen the CEO's calls and not the purchaser of promotional items.

6. **Don't persuade, qualify!**

7. **Know what you'll say to differentiate yourself**
   Promote what you are good at.

8. **Pursue only qualified prospects**
   Qualify prospects and only deal with them.

Marketing to End buyers

End-buyer initiative
Start attending marketing classes and sow seeds at schools, colleges, high schools and universities. You should do initiatives at universities to tell them that promotional items are becoming an extremely competitive media.

Self-promotions
Hand out your own gifts to promote yourself when you visit a company.

End-buyer shows
This is also attending shows that your prospective client would and do handouts or a marketing initiative for these prospective clients.

Web research and warm calls
Look at client's websites so that you know about their business before you contact them. At least when you call them, you will know a little about their business.

What do you do for a living?
Always know how to answer this question. Move from selling stuff to integrated marketing plans.
Selling stuff = purchase department = price
Sell outcomes = decision makers = margin

Integrated marketing plan = the road map that will take your client to meeting their objectives. A schedule showing all marketing activities such as promotions, programs, trade shows, print, radio, TV, events etc. Do a schedule that shows dates and items that need to be ordered for an event. Put the event in the schedule as well as items that support these ideas and the costs.

There are 4 types of distributor sales people
Order takers = wait for the phone call or email
Order getters = hey, what to buy some pens?
Order makers = what about those trade shows? Let's get things ordered in advance.
Marketing strategists = I noticed on your website that you plan to exhibit at 23 trade shows next year. What are your desired outcomes? What is your life time value of a client?
Which would you prefer to be?

How Things Work – Understanding Artwork and Printing

It is important for your client's image that their corporate brand or identity is always consistent.

Many suppliers offer in-house art and design services for a fee. In many cases, creating art is as simple as utilising services that are already in place.

Art vs. Artwork

While art may be considered anything that is creative and artistic, artwork adheres to accepted guidelines and professional procedures (sometimes called standards) so that suppliers can reproduce it, either on paper or on a variety of promotional products.

When re-creating an existing company logo, the goal is to duplicate the original as precisely as possible.

It is extremely important to obtain client approval on a paper copy (proof) that depicts the logo as it is to be imprinted, spelling out each colour exactly before the job is printed.

Who Owns the Art?

Chances are your client owns all rights in and to his or her logo.
This means that you can only reproduce that logo on a promotional item with the full consent and permission of your client.

To avoid possible copyright issues when contracting an artist to create an advertising logo or message for you or your client, it is a good idea to use a "work for hire" agreement.

Electronic Arts Formats Explained

It's a good idea to "achieve" your client's art and logo by saving it in several electronic formats. Make sure that each contains the company name and contact information.

- **VECTOR GRAPHIC FILE** is a method of image generation using a number of straight lines and/or arcs of different length and angular orientation. This format is highly recommended, as it offers the most flexibility and is used by most promotional product suppliers. Commonly used programs include CorelDraw and Adobe Illustrator. Vector files should be saved in their native format with embedded fonts and also as both an esp. file and PDF file with fonts converted to curves or paths.

- **A BITMAP** is a digital representation of an image where a grid is used to indicate whether each point of the image black, white or a colour. If a logo or message has been created as a bitmap (or your existing logo as been scanned), save the file in its native format, for example: .bmp, .tif or .pct. For this file to be considered acceptable, it must be at least 100% of the printed size for black and white images and 200% of size for colour. Popular bitmap manipulation programs include Adobe Photoshop, and Corel Photo paint.

These programs will also usually require a recreation of logos at an additional cost.

Can't you just get the logo from our website?

Probably not...at least not without additional charges. Graphics on websites are designed to load as fast as possible, and usually lack sufficient quality for reproduction on promotional products. While web graphics may be adapted to work, it may very well involve recreating the logo, which will almost certainly result in additional costs.

Industry Charges and Buzzwords

Like most industries, the promotional products industry has its own unique terms and buzzwords. Even the most seasoned professionals may sometimes fail to fully explain what they mean.

This section is designed to provide you with basic information that will help you to better communicate with your clients and suppliers to achieve the results you desire. It covers just a few of the most common terms and decorating processes. Keep in mind; this is an area that changes rapidly with technological advances. Your best suppliers can guide you through the maze of decorating techniques to ensure that your client's logo or message is presented in the most favourable manner.

Common Setup Procedures and Charges

- **CAMERA READY ARTWORK** – the traditional reference to artwork that is complete and ready to use without further modification. "Camera Ready" often consists of a black image on white paper, exactly 100% of the printed size, on high-quality photographic paper. While many office laser printers are capable of creating acceptable results, most ink jet printers are not. Remember, the final result will depend entirely on the quality of the artwork.

- **COLOUR SEPERATIONS** – With multi-colour artwork, there is a separate piece of camera ready art for each printed colour, and registration marks on each sheet to ensure that all the colours line up to create the desired result.

- **FILM** – Camera ready art is often scanned or actually photographed to create either a film positive or a film negative that may be used in the creation of a screen or die. It more closely resembles the film of an X-ray than the film of a small camera.

- **SPOT COLOUR** – Each specific colour of ink is printed right where it's needed. What you see is what you get. For example, if you are printing a three colour logo of green, blue and yellow, only green, blue and yellow ink would be used.

- **PROCESS COLOUR** – This process mixes the four basic colours of cyan, magenta, yellow and black (CMYK) to create nearly any colour allowing for the appearance of a "full colour" imprint, using just four basic colours of ink.

- **ELECTRONIC ARTWORK** – a computer generated file of artwork everything necessary to generate colour separated, camera ready art.

- **SETUP COST** – The charge to make a job ready for production.

- **COLOUR MATCH CHARGE** – The cost to mix inks to match a specific colour. The industry standard for colour matching is the "Pantone" or "PMS" colour matching system.

Methods of Decoration

Here is a brief overview of the most common processes used to decorate promotional products, along with their pros and cons:

- **SCREEN PRINTING**: Setup involves using a combination of light and chemicals to "burn" the image into a pattern on the screen. The screens are then set up and registered, and ink is then physically pushed through the pattern in the screen to imprint the design on a promotional product. The ink may then be "cured" by running the printed item under a heating element.

    o **PROS**: Screen printing is relatively quick, affordable and long lasting. It can reproduce fine detail, colour matching, and can be used on many surfaces, including glassware and textiles.

    o **CONS**: With spot colour printing, each colour requires an additional screen and/or set up, often resulting in additional charges. Process colour printing is possible, but colour separations can be very costly, and getting a correct, consistent finished result can be tricky. Flash curing individual inks may also be necessary when printing colour on colour (particularly white on dark items.) This may result in additional "flash" charges.

- **PAD PRINTING**: Setup involves rendering the image onto a rubber pad template, similar to a soft rubber "stamp". Ink is then transferred from the rubber pad onto the promotional product.

o **PROS**: Pad printing can be used to print on irregular surfaces, like golf balls or even walnuts. Colour matching is also possible.

o **CONS**: Multiple colour printing is not always possible, and pad printing is best suited to smaller imprint areas.

- **EMBROIDERY**: Setup involves telling an embroidery machine exactly where to place each stitch. Thread is sewn into a pattern, creating the logo or message.

    o **PROS**: Embroidery is perceived as an "upscale" option, providing a rich and sophisticated look.

    o **CONS**: It is not always possible to reproduce fine detail or shading in an embroided logo. In some cases, modification of the logo may be necessary. "Digitization", "punching" or "tape" charges (embroidery setup) can be more expensive than other types of setup charges. These costs are usually based on the number of stitches (i.e. larger designs mean more stitches and a higher price.)

- **OFFSET PRINTING:** Setup involves the creation of a plate or template. An inked image is set off from a printing plate onto a rubber blanket which in-turn is transferred to paper.

    o **PROS:** The process provides exact reproduction, and is inexpensive in larger runs.

    o **CONS:** Offset printing is limited to flat paper products.

- **TRANSFER PRINTING:** In this process, transfers are created, utilizing special printers and sublimation inks. Heat and pressure transfer the image onto the promotional product.

o **PROS:** Full colour is possible, and digital printing allows this to be done, even in smaller quantities.

o **CONS:** Cannot be used on all surfaces. Limited to use on promotional products designed to receive sublimation inks (i.e. certain t-shirts, glassware, mugs, mouse pads and plaques.)

- **ETCHING AND ENGRAVING:** Setup may involve creating a template or programming the laser (or other equipment) on where to cut. In this process, a hand tool, chemical, laser or abrasive is used to remove material and etch or cut the logo or message into the product. This process can be used on a variety of materials including metal, glass, stone and wood.

    o **PROS:** Beautiful, three-dimensional look.

    o **CONS:** Setup can be costly, and no colours are involved, unless another decoration process is also used.

- **HOT STAMPING, EMBOSSING AND DEBOSSING:** Setup begins with production of a metal die, and costs vary according to size. The die is used to press the logo or message into the promotional item.

    o **PROS:** These processes provide excellent results on vinyl, leather and even some paper products.

    o **CONS:** It is not always possible to reproduce fine detail or shading using these processes.

BEST PRACTICES WITHIN THE PROMOTIONAL PRODUCTS INDUSTRY

The two core players in this supply chain are supplier companies who design, source, manage, and imprint promotional products; and marketing distributors who promote, sell, and distribute these products. In the supply chain, each relies heavily on the other for critical business functions.

Best practices for promotional products SUPPLIERS
Communications

- ❏ Create a customer-centric focus on phone communications. As the primary interactive tool between suppliers and distributors, train your team to be the best phone service agents in the industry. Maximise your use of voice mail by adopting a system that provides easy usability and maintains strong, open communications.
- ❏ Set communications standards for your team that provide targeted metrics for responding to distributors. Adopting specific metrics such as time frames for returning phone calls, emails, and acknowledging the receipt of artwork and purchase orders offers a consistent, open dialog to customers.
- ❏ Take on the role of educator and advisor. Distributors look to you as their experts in your product category. They welcome your advice and knowledge in all aspects of your business – on product, artwork, sales, and imprinting. Those suppliers who take on these roles report the strongest relationships with distributors.
- ❏ Confirm verbal quotes in writing. Whether it's via fax or email, provide a written record for the distributor and your staff.
- ❏ Clearly communicate all applicable charges and policies. As a production based operation, you offer a host of available value added services, each with its own fee structure and operational policies. Outline these clearly in your catalogue and on your website.

- Adopt a proactive approach to problem solving. When issues arise, advise the distributor immediately, seek consensus, and be prepared to offer options.
- Recognise that distributors are primarily service based organisations. As such, they act as middlemen in the sales channel and may require additional time to communicate with their customers. Be flexible and plan accordingly.

Order management
- Provide a written or electronic acknowledgement for every order placed. This document offers your understanding of the order and allows the distributor to verify the accuracy of the order details.
- Track all conversations with your distributor client. Accurately noting all conversations and changes will help your team stay organised and prioritise the details. The end result will be service to your customer.

Artwork and imprinting
- Clearly communicate your artwork requirements. The nuances of crisp, clean artwork require great attention to detail. Make these clear and specific to distributors and be prepared to train them in the details of your imprinting processes.
- Provide a written or electronic confirmation that artwork has been received. Verify that it meets your quality standards and that you have aligned it with the correct distributor purchase order.

Finance
- Utilise industry credit reporting services. These reports provide a current snapshot of distributor payment histories and will help you make more sound credit decisions.
- Forward invoices in a timely manner. While naturally a critical factor in your firm's cash flow, getting invoices to distributors also activates the net terms of your purchase agreement. For

faster processing, consider making invoices available in multiple formats.

Sales and Marketing

- ❏ Develop marketing tools that are also end-user friendly. Providing these tools in a way that can be presented to a distributor's customer will increase sales opportunities. An end user friendly tool is one that provides no direct supplier contact information. Such tools include flyers, catalogues and websites.
- ❏ Engineer these tools to allow distributors to customise them. Many distributors re-label these tools with their own branding, resulting in more buyers seeing your product.
- ❏ Date all marketing materials for easy reference.
- ❏ Build a case history library for your best selling products. Case histories are selling stories that describe unique ways of how others have successfully used your product. They are proven tools that positively influence buying decisions. Make your stories available in multiple formats.
- ❏ Create a digital image library of your entire product line. Offering a file of each product – down to the size and colour with no logo. This will allow distributors to expand their own marketing reach. Distributors proactively use these files for their own catalogue, website, and virtual sample programs. Virtual samples alone go along way to finalising the buying decision and eliminate the cost of imprinting a physical speculative sample.
- ❏ Position your products by selling benefits over features. Benefits provide distributors with specific information about what makes your product so useful and how it can be applied to specific marketing challenges. Case studies are a popular way to communicate this and will also identify which markets and industries have successfully used your product. In contrast, promoting your product solely on its features, its basic characteristics such as size or colour, does not offer the most advantageous buying scenario.

Technology

- Provide online order and shipping status. Distributors spend a considerable amount of time tracking the progress of their orders and providing an online venue allows them to respond faster to their customer.
- Keep your website relevant and up-to-date. This is your most fluid marketing and communication tool to distributors. Many distributors have come to rely on this tool to get many of the answers they are looking for, day or night.

Delivery

- Provide realistic delivery schedules that you can commit to. Many orders are time sensitive and have a specific in-hands use date. If a committed delivery date can not be met, advise the distributor immediately and be prepared to provide options.
- Once delivered, provide an electronic format for advising delivery information.

Communications
Best Practices for PROMOTIONAL DISTRIBUTORS

Communications

- Be responsive and accessible to inquiries made by suppliers. Their communications to you generally indicate a question or issue about your order and, pending an answer from you, places your order on hold until you instruct them on how to proceed.
- Provide complete contact details on every purchase order. This includes the sales person's information as they are most often in the best position to answer any questions. Also provide an alternate contact, such as a support person.
- Consult your supplier's catalogue or web site for any initial questions you have. Most information is there and may save you both time and money.

Order Management

- ❏ Provide a complete, accurate, and thorough purchase order. Industry studies show that as many as two-thirds of distributor orders arrive at a supplier incorrect, that is, they are missing some piece of information that requires some type of follow up action.
- ❏ Provide complete contact details on every purchase order. This includes the phone, fax, and e-mail of a primary contact person to whom all questions can be directed.
- ❏ Track all conversations with your supplier. Accurately noting all conversations and changes will help your team stay organized and prioritize the details. The end result is better service to your customer.
- ❏ Be specific about the true required "in hands" date of your order. Padding an in-hands date impacts your supplier's production pipeline and may incur additional charges. Many suppliers primarily schedule their production flow using these dates, so avoid specifying "ASAP".
- ❏ Recognize that suppliers are primarily manufacturing-based operations. As such, they are the production arm of the sales channel and focus heavily on the details and logistics of manufacturing. Making changes to orders in a production pipeline requires time and there is often a cost associated with it. Be flexible and communicate this to your customers.

Artwork & Imprinting

- ❏ Learn everything that you can about the printing process, it will help you communicate your needs better with your customer, and help you manage the dynamics of the dozens of imprint methods offered today.
- ❏ Become an expert in the imprinting processes of your top suppliers. Let your supplier teach you about their processes, their imprinting dynamics, and their challenges to creating great imprinting.
- ❏ Become an expert in the electronic artwork requirements of your top suppliers. Each will detail these specifications in their

catalogue and/or web site and meeting these requirements early on will not only save time and money but will yield the best imprinting results.

- Provide complete contact and order details when sending artwork electronically. Since this is often done to a separate supplier e-mail address, this should include your primary contact, company, and e-mail information as well as your phone, fax, and purchase order numbers.
- Train your staff in the Pantone Matching System (PMS). PMS is a numerical colour matching system that classifies colours into families of colour stories. PMS has become an integral part of the industry and understanding the nuances of colour is critical to your company's success.
- Submit a hard copy of your artwork together with your PO. Since electronic art files can become corrupt during transmittal, a PDF or fax will provide an accurate, proportional representation of the required imprint.
- Review paper/electronic proofs from your supplier carefully. This includes spelling, layout, and design elements. Respond quickly with any changes and detail specifically how these edits should be made.

Finance

- Take good care of your credit rating. There is an industry credit rating service and suppliers make regular submissions of poor payment histories which are accessible to other suppliers. Suppliers make conscious credit decisions based on your past payment history.
- Pay your invoices within the agreed upon terms. Net 30 Days is the industry standard, however, you may be able to negotiate other terms with your supplier. Likewise, paying your supplier only after your customer has paid you is not an acceptable practice.
- Understand that communication is key in resolving credit issues. Such issues are commonplace in the industry so help your supplier understand your situation.

Sales & Marketing

- ❏ Learn to use supplier-developed marketing tools. Suppliers are experts at presenting their product and have absorbed the costs of creating these tools for you. The best tools – catalogues, flyers, web sites, and samples, for example – will be end-user friendly and offer your team a no-cost avenue to increasing sales and profitability.
- ❏ Give suppliers access to your sales team. These individuals have been trained to discuss the best applications for their product and focus on providing case histories of how their product works best in specific markets. They are a valuable training resource for product, artwork, imprinting, and sales information.
- ❏ Support regional and national trade shows. Suppliers invest heavily in providing your team a central venue – a large showroom, so to speak – for product ideas, inspiration, and education.

Technology

- ❏ Learn to use the enabling technologies of your top suppliers. Based on sheer numbers, many suppliers will process a factor of perhaps 10-15 times the volume of orders, sales calls, and artwork files of your firm in a given year and therefore must automate some of their functions. As a result, such tools as online order tracking, digital artwork proofing, virtual sampling, and automated phone attendants can be valuable ways for you to manage your orders.
- ❏ Adopt Standards for order processing. The ePromoStandardsAlliance is an industry body that has developed key communications technologies for electronically transmitting order information between suppliers and distributors. Depending on the size of your firm, you may be able to realize added efficiencies in order processing.

Delivery

- ❏ Be very specific with your selected method of delivery. Contact your supplier for any questions about what the best delivery options may be. Depending on the product, the supplier can advise you on alternative methods that may be more timely or cost effective.

❑ Verify and validate your delivery address. The slightest error can affect the timely delivery of your client's order. As a rule, carriers charge the actual shipper (the supplier) and not the "third party" for errors in addresses.

JOINT BEST PRACTICES FOR SUPPLIERS & DISTRIBUTORS

❑ Develop a code of ethics for your firm. Train your team in fair business practices, respectful communications, and mutual problem resolution.

❑ Take responsibility for your mistakes. It is understood that mistakes will happen, however, how your team handles these situations is what can set you apart from others.

❑ Provide extensive training for new employees and continuing education for current staff. Core topics should include the industry, product, imprinting, the customer, and communications. Providing a solid initial knowledge base means a more consistent delivery of customer service.

❑ Be respectful of each other's place in the supply chain. Both suppliers and distributors face challenges unique to their role in the industry. The greatest partnership successes occur when both sides are understanding and respectful of these dynamics.

Emailing suppliers

Subject
Every email message has a "subject" that should contain your distributor company name and purchase order number associated with your artwork file attachment.
Example: Artwork for Delbi Promotions – PO #3825

Signatures
Do not be anonymous! Suppliers need to know who is sending the artwork, and the email reply address is often misleading or insufficient. Be sure to sign your email messages with all of these details:

- Full name of the sender or contact regarding the artwork
- Your company name
- The physical address of your company and/or the sender
- Your email address (for all reply messages)
- Telephone and fax numbers

Message Body
Take the time to make your email messages as detailed as possible to avoid confusion and delays. It helps to state the number of attached files, as in these examples:

- "Enclosed are two artwork files, one for each side of the mug."
- "Enclosed is one ZIP archive containing three font files, one Photoshop image, two CorelDraw illustrations and my document"

Compression
Before sending the artwork file, you should use compression software to protect against damage-in-transit. Compression can make large files smaller to decrease the online transfer time, but the most important benefit is the way it encloses the delicate artwork files inside a file type that was designed for proper transmittal. The two most popular compression formats are .zip.

Best wishes
I hope that you have discovered real tools to assist you in your business.

Delia Biljon